First Book of Knowledge

David Roberts

Sundial

Photographs at the front of this book:

(Endpapers) Forests provide us with one of our most important materials – wood. Each year, an enormous number of trees are cut down or *felled,* like those shown in the picture, which have been cut with a powerful chain saw.

(Title pages) Some of the many spectacular hot-air balloons that took part in an international race in Mexico.

(Contents pages) An experienced team of climbers practise a mountain rescue operation. The 'injured climber' in this exercise is a dummy, strapped in red protective sheeting to a type of stretcher.

CONTENTS

First published 1977 by
Sundial Books Limited
59 Grosvenor Street
London W1

© 1977 Hennerwood Publications Limited

ISBN 0 904230 38 4

Printed in Great Britain by Jarrold & Sons Limited

INTRODUCTION

About a hundred years ago, a famous writer of children's stories called Robert Louis Stevenson had a happy thought:

> *The world is so full*
> *of a number of things,*
> *I'm sure we should all*
> *be as happy as kings.*

He wrote it down so that, a hundred years later, you could read it. A hundred years is a long time, and the world is a big place. It must be even more full of a bigger number of things than it was when Robert Louis Stevenson thought about it.

For that is the really wonderful thing about the world. However many things there are in it, there always seems to be room for more. Which is just as well when you think how fast we're adding to the world's collection of things.

The world is a great collector. Until we came along, it took its time about amassing its collection. It took two thousand million years to collect itself together into the great globe we call planet Earth. It took another thousand million years to put the parts together to make the first living things, those strange, microscopic things, part plant, part animal, we call bacteria. Another thousand million years had passed before chlorophyll appeared and that made the green plants possible.

Since then, the pace has quickened. The world's collection of plants and animals has increased in numbers and variety to an extent hard even for us to imagine. For instance, there are nearly two hundred and fifty thousand flowering plants known to us and more are being discovered all the time. We have classified one hundred and fifty thousand different species of moths and butterflies, and we're not at the end of the list.

Many items have been dropped from the catalogue of the world's collection. For millions of years, giant reptiles ruled the world. Now only their skeletons turned to stone are left for us to look at and wonder. Every few years, some species disappear for ever and the room left for others dwindles.

We are newcomers in this world. With our present upright, almost hairless bodies and with our keen, inventive brains, we have been here for about forty thousand years. For most of that time, we were just another animal in the world's collection. Then, only about five thousand years ago did we get together in large enough numbers to make much difference to the world as we found it.

Since that time, we have added more and more to the world's collection of wonders. So inventive and active have we been that we have forgotten a lot of what we did in the past. In recent years we have begun to learn about the cities built and the civilizations planned by our remote ancestors. Often, we have been too ready to tear down what went before to make room for our new schemes for a perfect world.

Only for about two hundred years have we been able to move about our world with any ease. Until we found a power to move our vehicles other than our own muscle or the muscle of the animals we tamed, travel overland was slow and uncertain. Ocean crossings were rare with our own fears and the uncertainties of wind and weather to overcome. Now, if we want to, we can reach any corner of the world in a matter of hours.

A good deal has happened in the past hundred years. Robert Louis Stevenson would hardly recognize our world. Yet he might find as many new things to make him happy as there are new things that might sadden him. He would like our new-found love of past things and our concern to preserve beautiful things. He would enjoy some of the new wonders the world has collected.

First Book of Knowledge is full of many things. It tells you about the world you live in as Nature has made it. It shows you how we have come to learn about our world, what changes we have made in it, what fun we can have in it and what skill we have brought to it.

It will take you on your first step into the world of knowledge — surely the most fascinating world of all.

THE WORLD ABOUT US

An enormous cloud of dust took two thousand million years to compress itself into a great solid ball. As it did so, it produced more than ninety different kinds of atoms. Pairs and groups of atoms combined to make the solids, liquids and gases which formed themselves into land, sea and air. By some four thousand six hundred million years ago, our planet Earth had been created.

Since then, the surface of the globe has never stopped changing. It has trembled and cracked under the pressures beneath it. Its oceans have advanced and retreated. Its continents have drifted and changed shape. Wind and rain, ice and snow, heat and cold have chipped away or built up its landscape. Different forms of life have come and gone, piling up their dead remains.

The process goes on still. We can see it all around us.

▶ Layers of soft mud were left behind by successive flooding over millions of years. Each layer was pressed into solid rock by the weight of new layers above it. Then wind and rain and a river current ate away at the rock to produce this landscape in Utah, USA.

▲ The way wind and rain eat away at rock is called erosion. Here, in Monument Valley in the south-west USA, rock was first laid down over millions of years by layers of mud from rivers. A dry period killed most of the plants, and the topsoil blew away. The rock underneath, broken up by hot sun and wind, soon became light enough to blow away too, leaving behind pillars of firmer rock. The fallen stones, called scree, piled around the pillars, are still too big to blow away.

▲ Layers of rock on land or under the sand of the seabed may seem thick and solid, but there is great heat and pressure beneath them. Sometimes this breaks through a weak point, as when a volcano erupts. Molten rock, called lava, cools and becomes solid. Some of it is broken up into dust or ash by the escaping gases and thrown hundreds of metres into the air. It settles and is pressed by its own weight into a rock called tuff, shown here on the Canary Islands in the Atlantic Ocean.

▶ Scientists have counted about 450 active volcanoes on land and another 80 on the ocean bed. These are all weak points in the earth's crust which can erupt at any moment. In November 1963, there was one such eruption under the sea off the south coast of Iceland. Volcanic ash was blasted through 100 fathoms (184 metres) of water and thousands of metres into the air. Molten lava piled up and cooled into solid rock to build a new island, called Surtsey, which is still growing.

Here, in Moon Valley, La Paz, in the South American republic of Bolivia, pillars have been carved out of the soft rock by erosion. Compare them with the pillars made from harder rock in Monument Valley, on page 12.

The main rock forming most of the world's land masses is called granite. Here, at Yosemite Park, USA, erosion has peeled it away, layer by layer, like the skins of an onion.

▼ The towering peak of the Matterhorn in Switzerland is a fairly young mountain in terms of the earth's great age. It was built up about 50 million years ago. All year round, it is covered in snow and ice which is slowly wearing it away. Its summit is 4477 metres (14,688 feet) above sea level.

▲ Heat and pressure deep underground have turned this rock at Carrara, Italy, into pure white marble. Now, it is quarried for buildings and for sculpture.

The different chemicals of which rocks are formed are called minerals. Many minerals contain metals. It is the particular mineral or mixture of minerals that gives rocks their colour. Some minerals have formed crystals, flat-sided shapes that fit together like building bricks. This 18th century Spanish earring is made from the metal gold and crystals called emeralds.

This 17th century Italian ring is made of gold and holds a polished crystal of amethyst. For thousands of years, men have used metals and coloured crystals to make ornaments like this.

One of the most valuable kinds of crystal is called diamond. It is made from carbon, the element left behind by the partial burning of wood. To become a diamond crystal, the carbon must undergo great heat and pressure deep in the ground. Sometimes, erosion brings diamonds to the surface. Here, in a South African diamond mine, men are digging a tunnel to find them.

There are two kinds of rock minerals, those which contain metals and those without. Metallic minerals are called ores. The metal is separated out by crushing and heating the ore. These crystals are called pyromorphite, one of the ores of the metal lead.

There has been some form of life on our planet for about 3500 million years. For the past 700 million years, there have been animals with hard skeletons that could leave behind visible traces of themselves buried deep inside rocks. These fish lived in a freshwater lake that suddenly dried up 210 million years ago.

Between 225 million and 75 million years ago, shellfish called ammonites were common in the oceans. When they died, their shells sank to the muddy bottom where they were covered by more mud. In time, the weight of the layers above enclosed them within solid rock. At various times, the level of the sea fell or the seabed was lifted above the water level by volcanic action. Now, ammonite fossils are found even on dry land far from the sea.

Here is a rock fossil of the reptile *Nothosaurus* which lived about 230 million years ago. Its skeleton is about 25 centimetres (9·8 inches) long. It spent most of its time in the sea, but the female came on to dry land to lay her eggs. Fossil remains of *Nothosaurus* have been found in Europe and Asia.

About 600 million years ago, there appeared on the seabed creatures called sea lillies or crinoids. They look rather like plants, but are really animals clinging to the seabed with a long, stemlike tail. The top has feelers waving in the water to gather food. This fossil is 14 centimetres long (5·5 inches) long. Crinoids still live in the sea, little changed over hundreds of millions of years.

This is the fossil of a fish called *Eobothus minimus,* an early flatfish like modern flounders. It measures 6 centimetres (2·4 inches).

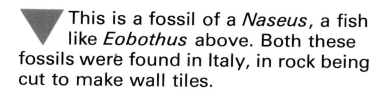

This is a fossil of a *Naseus*, a fish like *Eobothus* above. Both these fossils were found in Italy, in rock being cut to make wall tiles.

▲ More than seven-tenths of the
Earth's surface is covered by sea.
Most of the world's living things are in
the sea. In the north and south polar
regions, very cold water from melting ice
and snow sinks to the bottom, carrying
down oxygen which can keep animals
alive even at the greatest depths.

▶ Plants in the sea are usually
very small. These are only
single plant cells called diatoms seen
through a microscope. The largest round
one is in reality only about 0·2
millimetres (0·0079 inches) across.

This Porpita might look like a plant, but is really a collection of animals living together in what is called a colony. The tentacles, which comb the water for food, are held near the surface by a gas-filled disc. The feeding animals live under this disc, where there are also plant cells to supply them with extra oxygen.

▶ Coral is made from the skeletons of tiny animals living in warm tropical oceans. Each living animal is attached to the skeletons of dead ancestors, building up to make reefs and even whole islands.

Here is part of a coral reef. The living animals of a coral reef, called polyps, have plant cells in their soft tissue. These provide oxygen from the process used for the growth of most plants, called photosynthesis. This process needs sunlight, so coral polyps can live only near the surface where light can reach them.

▶ Here is another kind of coral. Each polyp has a ring of tentacles which gather very tiny animals called plankton into the central mouth. At the base of the polyp is a skeleton attached to the skeletons of dead polyps below. As the polyps live, give birth to new ones and die, the coral reef is built up. Large kinds like these grow slowly, the smaller, branching types more rapidly.

▲ Small fish, like these *Haemulon,*
often move about in great numbers
called shoals. Big or small, the ocean's
inhabitants live on plants or other
animals, each being part of a long food
chain. The food chain starts with the tiny
plants like the diatoms on page 22.

Many different kinds of animals, both on land and in the sea, can grow a hard outer covering or shell. This protects the soft body of the animal inside. Many different animals with shells are called molluscs. As the mollusc grows, so does its shell covering. Material to make the shell comes from the food the mollusc eats, which also gives it its colour. Shells grow ridges and sometimes horny spines, like those on this arthritic spider conch from the coral reefs of East Africa and the Indian Ocean.

▶ Gastropods are a group of molluscs with a single shell and a muscular foot on which they move about. Often, this foot has a hard base which closes the shell when the soft body is drawn up inside. This limpet clamps its foot to a rock, drawing its shell down on to it to resist the pull of the waves.

▼ Beneath the coloured pattern of this shell is a thick layer of mother-of-pearl, once used to make pearl buttons. It was almost hunted out of existence until plastic replaced pearl for buttons.

This giant frilly clam has two shells hinged at one side. The opposite edges fit tightly together when the shell is closed, as it is here. This kind of mollusc is called a bivalve, meaning two shells. Its rather flat foot pokes out between the shells to burrow into the sand, where most bivalves live.

This Atlantic sundial shows clearly how a single-shelled mollusc or gastropod grows in a spiral. As the soft body inside grows in length, so more shell is added in widening circles. This is a very flat variety. Sometimes, the spiral is tall and narrow.

A seashell has three layers. The two outer ones grow round the opening. The inner layer grows all over the inside surface, thickening the shell. In this triumphant star, the inner layer is mother-of-pearl and so are the hollow spines round the edge. As each coil grows round the one before, the spines are dissolved away, leaving only tiny traces on the shell's surface.

The variety in the shells of sea animals gives us some of Nature's most beautiful objects to collect from the beach. The chalky substance that has built up chalk hills and cliffs is also made from tiny animals and plants.

PLANTS AND ANIMALS

When the Earth was first formed, it was surrounded by a mixture of gases, but no free air or oxygen. Plants and animals cannot live without oxygen, so there was no life on Earth. It was the heat of the sun that separated oxygen from water vapour and nitrogen from ammonia to make the air we breathe today. The sun's heat created big molecules called proteins, the building bricks of living things.

Microscopic living things called bacteria began to appear three thousand, five hundred million years ago. About 1000 million years later, chemical reactions caused by the sun led to the formation of chlorophyll, the green substance that makes the food for growing plants. Microscopic plants, and animals that could feed on them, appeared in the oceans. More than four hundred million years ago, plants began to thrive on dry land. Then animals climbed ashore to feed on them.

The battle for life has gone on ever since. The process, called 'evolution' has created the millions of living things in our world, including, eventually, man.

▶ Man is the most successful animal at adapting Nature's laws to his use. He has learned how to breed a perfect red point Siamese kitten and to cultivate Pelargoniums (or geraniums as they are better known) with large, long-lasting, colourful blooms.

To survive on land, most plants must have sunlight which the chlorophyll in their leaves uses to help make their food. This bird's nest fern grows large, broad leaves, fanned out to capture as much sunlight as possible.

Ferns do not have flowers and seeds. They reproduce from new shoots and from tiny spores which are formed under their leaves. The spores are scattered by the wind to where new plants can grow from them

This chameleon or earth star gets its share of sunlight by growing on the highest branches of trees in tropical forests. Plants like this one that grow on other plants are called epiphytes.

This is the curly fern or sword fern. Its many tiny leaves grow on long, curling stems which hang down all around it. By this means, it makes sure that, all day, some of its leaves are turned directly towards whatever sunshine there is.

▲ A fungus, like this very poisonous fly agaric, has no chlorophyll with which to make its own food. It feeds on decaying matter from other plants and animals. Most of a fungus is underground. The part you see is a kind of fruit containing the spores from which new plants grow.

▶ This is the horse mushroom. It looks like the field mushroom we eat and can itself be eaten. It is safest, though, never to eat fungus that has been gathered growing wild. Many kinds are poisonous.

▲ These are field mushrooms. The picture shows the stages through which the fruiting part grows and develops its umbrella shape. The lines on the underside of the fully grown mushroom are the gills which bear the millions of tiny dust-like spores which will eventually fall out and be scattered by the wind. A few, but only very few, will settle where a new fungus may grow. This is Nature's way of making sure the species will survive.

► This is a bracket fungus. The hidden part grows deep into the rotting wood on which it feeds. The spores develop on the shelf-like structures shown here.

▲ The biggest non-flowering plants are the coniferous trees, so called because their seeds are produced in cones. Cones can be seen growing on this noble fir from the north-west United States of America. They are clusters of tightly packed scales which become hard and woody. The seeds appear between these leafy scales and are never completely enclosed. When they are ripe, they fall out and begin the growth of a new tree. It is often many years before a young tree begins to produce cones and seeds. Trees like this grow very tall.

Another conifer is the Scots pine, shown here growing beside a Scottish loch. Like most conifers, pines have very small, slender leaves called needles. These do not all drop off in the autumn. For this reason, they are called evergreens. The needle shape of the pine leaf helps to prevent it losing moisture through its breathing holes. The tree can, therefore, live in fairly dry places, like the rocky slopes of mountains where the rain runs away quickly.

▲ About 150 million years ago, Nature evolved a new kind of seed producer, the flower. Flowering plants adapted themselves to all sorts of weather conditions. They spread over almost all the land and created nearly a quarter of a million varieties. This fuschia grows in the mountains at the southernmost tip of South America.

◀ At first, flowers scattered their pollen in the wind. Then insects came along to carry pollen from flower to flower. The flowers grew bigger and brighter to attract insects. These pasque flowers have mauve petals and yellow centres where the pollen is produced. The sweet smell and sugary nectar also attract the insects to the flowers.

Flowering plants have become successful by protecting their seeds as they grow. Ferns and fungi produce millions of spores of which only a small number grow into new plants. Even conifers produce dozens of seeds, yet only a few survive. Some flowering plants have seed-cases in which the seeds are protected during development. Colonies of flowering plants can spread rapidly like the dandelions which have covered this field with a bright yellow carpet.

Seeds of flowering plants are spread by various means with animals, water and wind all playing a part. Each dandelion seed is attached to a wisp of down which the wind can catch and float away. If you have ever blown a dandelion clock – which is made up of hundreds of individual seeds – you will have seen them dancing lightly in the breeze and noticed how far they travel before settling on the ground.

▲ These are flowers of the calico bush of North America. They grow in clusters. The stamens which produce the pollen are like the spokes of an umbrella. When a bee or other insect lands on a flower, the stamens spring up towards the centre, dusting the insect's furry body with pollen which is then carried to another flower.

◀ Different flowering plants have become adapted to life in different places. These are flowers of the common thrift or sea pink, adapted to life close to the sea and the salt spray. Other kinds of thrift are found on mountains or heathlands far from the sea.

These are flowers of a tree called the shrubby willow. They are really tight clusters of the inside parts of flowers with no petals – they are called catkins. There are male catkins which produce pollen from their stamens and female catkins that produce seeds in seedcases called carpels. Most willows have the male and female catkins on different trees. Pollen is carried from the male stamens to the sticky stigmas at the tips of the female carpels. A single grain of pollen landing on a stigma sends a tube down into the carpel to fertilize a seed. Other trees, like hazels, birches and oaks, have catkins. These are usually pollinated by the wind, but willows are pollinated by insects.

▼ Many trees have flowers with petals. These are the flowers of the gean or wild cherry. When the seed has been fertilized, the carpel swells to form a fleshy cherry around it. The seed is protected inside a hard, woody case called the stone. This kind of fruit is called a drupe. Juicy fruits with several seeds inside them and with no stone are called berries.

As we have seen with the conifers on pages 36 and 37, some trees are evergreens and never lose all their leaves. Other trees shed all their leaves in winter and grow new ones the following spring. Trees that shed all their leaves are called deciduous. Most deciduous flowering trees grow new leaves before their flowers appear. Others, like this Himalayan tulip tree, flower on bare twigs before the leaf buds open.

These are the flowers of one of the hundred varieties of *Bomarea.* They bloom in the tropical areas of South America where they have adapted to climbing or scrambling up through the taller shrubs and trees to get light.

Garden roses have all been bred over many years from the much smaller, wild species. This rose, called Peace, was produced by F. Meilland in his rose nursery at Cap d' Antibes in the south of France in the 1940s and is now grown in most countries of the world.

Red poppies grow wild in many parts of the world. This blue poppy is a cultivated garden species. The picture clearly shows the pollen-producing stamens gathered round the central column of fused carpels which will eventually swell and form the familiar seedcase of all poppies.

This is the flower of the sacred lotus which grows in shallow water. It has become famous from wall paintings and other decorations from ancient Egypt. In fact, it comes from India and was not introduced to Egypt until the 6th century BC. It has long been thought of as the flower sacred to the great religious leader, Buddha. It is also important for its food value. The seeds, leaves and root are all prepared and eaten in various ways, and the stamens are used for flavouring tea. There is an old legend about an island where visitors who have once eaten the sacred lotus lose all desire to return home.

46

This is one of the many varieties of greenhouse carnations. Many new colours and shapes of flowers have been created by gardeners and plant breeders. They take the pollen from the stamens of one flower and carefully place it on the stigma of another. The seed that results grows into a cross between the two flowers and is called a hybrid. Sometimes, but not often, hybrids develop naturally. Usually, pollen from one flower will be accepted only by another flower of the same kind. Interference by gardeners and scientists in this natural process has produced most of the fine blooms seen today.

▲ There is a great variety of cactus plants. This one, called *Parodia sanguiniflora,* has bright red flowers in summer. Its spherical body is the stem which holds its reserve of water. The spikes are the leaves, so small that very little water is lost.

◄ A miniature indoor garden can be very attractive. This one is planted in a large, shallow bowl. The plants here are called succulents. They have thick leaves which hold a lot of water, so the garden doesn't need watering very often and only a little at a time. This kind of plant should have its roots in a mixture of sand and peat. Stone chippings and pebbles make the garden look like the desert where these plants come from.

49

One way to grow indoor plants that need moisture and warmth is to plant them in a bottle. Wash and drain the bottle dry. Make long-handled tools with a fork and spoon tied to sticks; a rammer from a cotton reel with a stick jammed in the hole. Put a layer of stones in the bottom of the bottle and cover with soil. Make holes in the soil and edge plants into position. Cover roots with soil and firm with rammer. Leave the bottle stoppered until mist clears. Water very rarely in small amounts.

Artificially dwarfed trees are called 'bonsai'. Plant a young tree seedling in a plastic cup in which holes have been punched with a knitting needle. During the first two years, cut off any roots that appear through the holes. In the second year, pinch off some of the branch tips to make the plant bushy and an interesting shape. When you transplant into a bowl, drape the roots over a stone so that only the tips enter the soil. Bonsai trees like this miniature chestnut take several years to produce.

Alpine plants spread very readily and need only a little soil and water to thrive. This wall has been built without any mortar between the stones, so that Alpine plants can be grown in the crevices.

Here, some old pieces of carved masonry have been arranged to provide stands at different levels for pot plants. This makes good use of a small area where taller plants or climbers might block out the sunlight.

Town gardens are often shaded by surrounding buildings. One way to get over this is to put plants in containers that can be moved into sunny positions, when they are ready to flower. Spreading plants like this make the most of available sun.

There have often been arguments about whether a tomato is a fruit or a vegetable. We cook them like vegetables and eat them in salads. To a botanist, a tomato is the kind of fruit called a berry. In the flower, a cluster of tiny carpels containing the seeds swells out to make the fruit. The seeds can be found inside the tomato when it is cut open.

There have been gardens ever since people learned to move plants from one place to another. Efforts to make plants bigger and better began with their use as food. If more food can be grown from a particular piece of ground, then the gardener will be rewarded. Fruits, like these grapes, have been improved to make more sugars from the sunlight and more juice for wine.

These hot peppers are easy to grow in a pot. The fruit can be used when it turns green or left to turn red. It can be eaten raw in salads or included in cooked dishes to add flavour. It is not the same as the plant whose seeds provide us with peppercorns.

Here is a collection of food plants, some of which are cooked as vegetables, though they may really be fruit. The red and green peppers, the tomatoes and the small marrows (called courgettes) on the top of the pile are all fruits. The carrots are the roots of the plant and can be described as true vegetables. It is the young flower heads of globe artichokes which are cooked and eaten.

During hundreds of millions of years, life on Earth has adapted to changing conditions. Many animals that once roamed the land or swam in the seas have long since disappeared. They are said to be extinct. Many of today's animals have lived in their present form for only a small part of the Earth's history. Some can be traced back to remote ancestors who have left behind fossil remains. This is a reconstruction of one extinct relative of the modern elephant. Scientists call it *Deinotherium.* Notice how its tusks curved inwards from the lower jaw, unlike the outward curving tusks in the upper jaw of the modern elephant.

▲ Many remains of extinct animals have been found in the asphalt pits in Rancho La Brea in California. This reconstruction shows how the area might have looked millions of years ago. A sabre-tooth tiger is shown attacking a mammoth, both now extinct.

▶ For millions of years, the Earth was dominated by giant reptiles called dinosaurs, like this *Stegosaurus* which is 6 metres (19 feet 8 inches) long. Protected by a powerful, spiked tail and stiff armoured plates along its back, it was a peaceful vegetarian browser.

One of the last giant dinosaurs was *Tyrannosaurus rex,* 6 metres (19 feet 8 inches) tall and 15 metres (49 feet 2·5 inches) from nose to tail. Its powerful jaws, crammed with sharp pointed teeth, could crush and tear both the smaller animals it fed on and its enemies.

Even insects once grew to be very big. This prehistoric dragonfly called *Meganeura* had a wingspan of almost 1 metre (3 feet 3 inches). The beating of its wings at the speed to lift it into the air must have made a tremendous noise.

▼ Life began in the oceans, and even today, most of the Earth's creatures live there. They have many different survival systems. This zebra scorpion fish is a slow swimmer. It lurks on the sandy bottom, looking like coral. When a victim comes too close, a jerk of its fins sends it forward for a short-distance snatch. The spines along its back are loaded with deadly poison. Usually, it need only raise them threateningly to frighten off an attacker.

▶ This beautiful emperor butterfly fish uses brilliant colour to warn off others of its species, like a flag of occupation. It lives along reefs in tropical waters. Each pair has its feeding territory. The black stripe across its eye helps to confuse the position of that organ, another way nature protects a vital part of an animal from sudden attack. Sometimes, even false eyes are included in an animal's colouring.

Often, the large and small in the animal world can live quite happily and usefully together. This is the whale shark. Despite its size, it is one of the most peaceful of fish. It lives by taking into its huge mouth water filled with the microscopic life called plankton. The water is filtered through gill-rakes leaving behind the food. Remora fish cling to its lower jaw, feeding from whatever spills from it and help the shark by eating parasites from its body.

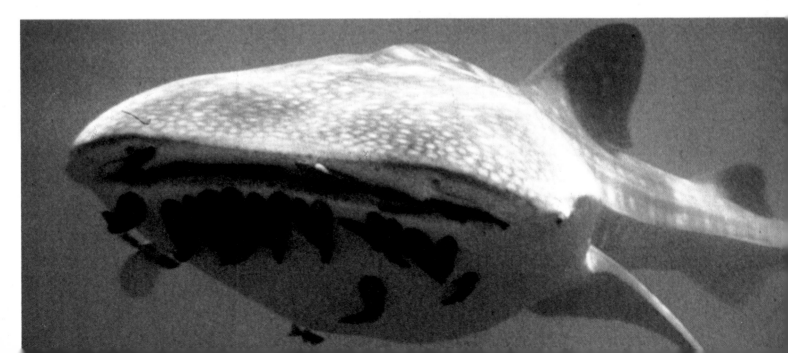

▶ Here is another butterfly fish, with the scientific name, *Chaetodon rafflesi.* It is one of over 200 different species. A pair of one species might claim more than 1 square kilometre (0·386 square mile) of coral reef. None of its own kind is allowed to invade it, though other species are ignored. Thus, a single stretch of reef can be brilliant with the colours of many different butterfly fish.

The lion fish from the Australian coral reefs spreads its spines to make itself as big and dangerous looking as possible to scare away enemies. In case that doesn't work, the spines are tipped with poison. Stripes are another device of nature to scare away enemies. They distort the outline, making an attacker uncertain what to expect.

This is an orange-striped trigger fish. Triggers get their name from a long spine on the back fitting into a groove. It can be raised and locked upright by a second spine behind it. Wedged into a crevice with the trigger raised, it cannot be pulled out by an enemy. Its tail also has a saw edge for attack. Triggers usually feed on spiny star-fishes and sea-urchins.

This is one of the angler fish; the adult fish live at a depth below 1000 metres (3280 feet). Its body is covered with long hairs that can detect the smallest movement in the permanent darkness of these depths. It also has a tuft on its head, called an esca, which lures its victims like the bait of a fishing line. In other species, the lure gives off light to spotlight the prey. This fearsome specimen is only 10 centimetres (3·9 inches) long.

Insects have lived on Earth almost as long as there have been food plants for them. In time, they learned to fly and to feed on each other. This female potter wasp has paralysed the caterpillar with her sting. She has dragged it to her clay nest and is stuffing it inside. When she has laid her eggs on the caterpiller, the nest will be sealed with more clay. The grubs can then hatch with a plentiful supply of caterpillar food on which to start life.

Perhaps the most popular insects are butterflies. When they begin to appear in the spring we know that the worst of the winter weather is over. In the picture is the purple-edged copper, widespread in Europe. It is found in boggy lowlands or up to heights of 1500 metres (5000 feet) in the mountains.

The acorn weevil is an odd looking beetle with a long snout. Its antennae grow from about halfway along this snout and its jaws are at the tip. The female bores a hole in an acorn and then turns round to lay one egg inside. The acorn provides the hatched larva with a supply of food.

▲ Bugs differ from beetles in having no distinct larva or pupa stage in their growth. The young are called nymphs. This plant-hopper is a nymph, having not yet grown wings. It has grown a tuft of waxy hairs, a peculiarity of some bugs.

▼ Flies are insects with only one pair of wings. The second pair have shrunk to small knobbed stalks called halteres which help to stabilize the insect in flight. This stalk-eyed fly has compound eyes on projections from the head which also carry short antennae.

Crickets have long thin antennae and make sounds by rubbing their wings together. Grasshoppers have short antennae and chirrup by rubbing their hindlegs against ridges on the wings. This male speckled bush-cricket, has wings reduced to small lobes.

Dragonflies and damselflies spend their early, larval stages in water. The damselfly has a weak, fluttering flight not at all like the powerful, darting flight of dragonflies. This damselfly is the common blue. It rests with wings folded not spread.

Reptiles have evolved from the first creatures to crawl out of the seas and lakes and take to life on dry land. Many are still amphibians which means they are equally at home in water or on land. Some, like frogs, toads, newts and salamanders, return to water to lay eggs. Their young have gills, like fish, for breathing under the water. They develop lungs as they grow up and climb on to the land. This is the green reed frog a rare African species.

This is called Wallace's flying frog. Its adult life is spent among the trees of Malaya. Its large, webbed feet act like parachutes when it leaps among the branches. It can glide quite long distances. It is named after Alfred Russel Wallace, the naturalist who first discovered it.

This is the eyed lizard, so called from the blue spots along its side. It is the largest European lizard, reaching 60 centimetres (23·6 inches) long. It is a reptile that lives on the ground, feeding on other lizards, small mammals, birds' eggs and fruit. Its eggs are laid in hollow trees or buried in the ground.

▲ This is the Indian gavial or gharial. It is one of several species of crocodiles and alligators which are among the most ancient of all surviving creatures. This one has long, slender jaws suitable for catching fish in the Ganges, Bramaputra and Indus rivers where it lives. Gavials can grow up to 3 metres (9·8 feet) in length but are not dangerous to humans.

Tortoises live on dry land. Turtles and terrapins live most of their time in water. They have been around for more than 200 million years. The land tortoise moves very slowly. Turtles can reach a speed of 15 knots in the sea. The picture shows a South African leopard tortoise enjoying a meal of cactus. Inside its bony shell, it breathes by the contraction and expansion of specially adapted muscles. Some turtles breathe underwater using a structure that works like the gills of a fish.

Not all snakes have poisonous fangs. This emerald tree boa is a constrictor which means that it crushes its victims in its coils. Unlike most snakes, boas have live young instead of laying eggs. Snakes are reptiles that no longer have legs, but they have learnt to move fast enough without them.

This chameleon from the mountains of Tanzania in Africa is one of a group of lizards that can change colour to match their surroundings. They move in slow motion and freeze in any position, though their tongues are incredibly swift to snatch their prey. Their eyes swivel independently.

Prehistoric gliding reptiles had wings of stretched skin. Then 160 million years ago, Nature invented feathers to make light wings and tails and to keep the creature warm. Birds need to be warm-blooded to develop the energy for flight. Birds became so successful that they spread throughout the world, even breeding in the icy wastes of Antarctica. This blue-headed tanager from America is skilled at catching insects on the wing.

There are two kinds of feathers: soft, downy ones and airtight and watertight ones. Waterfowl have particularly oily feathers to protect them in water. This mandarin duck is often seen on lakes in parks.

A bird needs to make a great effort to take off and to stay aloft. There is a lot of wear and tear on the feathers. Every year, some of them moult and new ones grow. Often, particularly in water birds, the power of flight is lost during the moulting season. Many birds take to flight reluctantly, preferring to run or swim away from danger. The biggest birds have lost the power of flight altogether. They have developed powerful legs instead, like this cassowary of Australasia and New Guinea. The bony helmet on its head protects it from thorns as it runs quickly through the brush.

▲ The long legs of the
Crowned Crane allow it to
wade through the African
marshes where it finds its
insect food. Here, it is shown in
a typical pose during a
courtship dance, in which the
bird hops, skips and jumps and
spreads its wings.

◀ This is the plum, or
blossom-headed,
parakeet from India and
eastwards to southern China. It
belongs to the parrot family,
with the familiar curved beak
for gathering and cracking the
seeds and nuts it eats.

▲ Among the most colourful parrots are those that live in tropical America. This red and green macaw is found from Panama to northern Argentina. Parrots are great fliers and don't really enjoy being caged.

◀ The soft feathers of owls make their flight almost silent when they swoop down at night to snatch up their prey. This barn owl is taking a brown rat back to its nest in an old church belfry tower.

▲ Warm-blooded animals were adapted to survive climatic change. Mammals have hair to keep warm, improved breathing systems and bigger brains than the reptiles they have replaced. They suckle their young, looking after them until they can fend for themselves. This lamb may have been born in a snowstorm, but its mother's care and milk help it to survive.

◄ Very large mammals have problems with their size and weight. The hippopotamus takes the weight off its feet by spending most of its time buoyed up in water. Babies are born in the rainy season in flattened reed nests and brought to the water in a few weeks. They soon become good swimmers, diving down to reach the mother's teats.

Early mammals were very small. Small mammals still thrive, particularly the many kinds of rodents. Among them are these field or short-tailed voles, very similar to mice and, indeed, once called grass mice. They live in fields, woodlands and even on moors. They may also come into gardens. They make roofed nests with shredded grass stems, hard to spot among surrounding dead grass and undergrowth.

Seals have developed thick, oily coats and heavy layers of fat which protect them from icy seas. This common seal is clumsy on land and spends most of its time in the sea, where it feeds on fish. Common seal babies shed their first white puppy coats before they are born and first face the world in their thick, adult coats. This is essential to a baby born on a rock or sandbank at low water and floated off by the rising tide.

▲ This young fallow deer can walk as soon as it is born. The mother gives it time to rest a lot at first, hidden by its dappled coat among brown leaves and shadows from overhead branches. But the youngster must be ready to follow the grazing herd as soon as possible.

▶ The tree kangaroo, like all marsupials or pouched animals, has another way of protecting its young. The baby spends its early months in the mother's pouch while she climbs among the branches feeding on leaves. The young of marsupials are very small, but grow quickly.

Early man was a hunter who learned about the animals he hunted. He found that some animals could be persuaded to live with him, as a walking milk supply or to carry his baggage. The donkey was bred from the wild ass as a beast of burden for man.

Even when they are not particularly useful, animals have amused us with their antics and have been kept as pets. All the golden hamster pets now so popular throughout the world are descended from a single family found wild in Syria in 1930.

Cats joined us about 5000 years ago. The lion was more common. Its power as the king of beasts made it an object of fear and awe, and its mane was a symbol of the sun. In the Middle East, the lion had a smaller cousin, the caffre cat. Where corn was gathered and stored, rats and mice were common pests. In pursuit of this prey, the caffre cat entered the human world. Ancient Egyptians worshipped it as a more tameable version of the lion. The Romans conquered Egypt and took over the cat as a household pet.

▶ The first white settlers in Australia enjoyed the antics of the wild budgerigar, shown here in its natural colours. One day, a Dr James White walked into a hut to be greeted with the words: "How d'you do, Dr White?" His assistant, Thomas Watling, had trained the first known talking budgie! Bred in a vast range of colours, it has become one of the world's favourite pets.

◀ Dogs first braved the glow of hunters' camp fires for scraps of food. They became bold enough to go with the hunters as they followed the grazing herds. The hunters learned to train dogs to chase their quarry towards their spears and arrows. Dogs have worked for us and befriended us ever since those times.

ARCHITECTURE

Long before the human animal appeared on Earth, other animals had taught themselves to build. Early man could watch the bird build its nest, the spider weave its web and the beaver construct its dam. With his superior brain and ability to make tools to help him, man could hope to do even better.

Other animals build for their immediate needs: a home to protect their young, a trap to collect food, a storehouse for the winter. Human beings build to last, often in the hope that their buildings will remain for ever. Many buildings that have lasted into our own day, may not be as they once were, but are still impressive enough for us to marvel at the work of our forefathers.

Alongside the skill of the builder, we value the art of the designer, the architect as we call him. Nowadays, we try to preserve examples from the past. They give us standards by which to judge modern architecture. Perhaps, they make us wonder which of our own buildings will be thought worthy of preservation by future generations.

◄ The ancient Romans learned to build from the Greeks. These pillars at the country palace of the Emperor Hadrian at Tivoli near Rome are copied from Greek architecture. Roman engineering skills brought water for the pool they surround.

▲ Many of the world's great buildings were designed as places of worship or to glorify a god. The pyramids of ancient Egypt, the first massive stone buildings, were mounds to cover the tombs of pharaohs, the godlike rulers of those times. The pyramid on the left covers the tomb of the Pharaoh Kephren. The Great Sphinx is believed to be his portrait. Pages 86 to 91 provide further examples of religious architecture.

◄ For people of the Moslem faith, the place of worship is called a mosque. One feature of a mosque is the minaret, a tower from which the faithful are called to prayer. This minaret, called the Malwiya, of the Great Mosque of Samarra in Iraq, was built in AD 848.

The ancient Romans were highly skilled at building arches and domes. This picture shows part of the dome of the Pantheon in Rome, built AD 118 to 128 and is 43·2 metres (142 feet) across. It is made of concrete, a mixture of gravel and cement, adjusted so that it becomes lighter in weight the nearer it is to the top. Before the invention of the dome, a roof covering this area needed the support of many pillars.

This is an ancient Greek temple called the Parthenon, built on the Acropolis, a hill overlooking Athens, between 447 and 438 BC. The Greeks knew about the arch but preferred the pillar and crossbeam method of supporting a roof. The Parthenon is built entirely of marble. At one time, the crossbeams above the pillars were decorated with marble sculptures. All that remains of them is now in the British Museum, London. The Parthenon is thought by some to be the most perfect building ever designed.

Two great world religions began in India, Hinduism and Buddhism. A Buddhist temple is a place of pilgrimage where relics of Buddha, who founded the religion, are kept. The main dome is called the stupa and is often surrounded by lesser shrines, as here in the Shwe Dagon temple in Rangoon, Burma.

This Hindu temple was built in the 12th century AD at Angkor Wat in Cambodia. It was originally designed as a temple to Suryavarman II, king of the Khmers, who was declared a god when he died. The central tower represents the sacred mountain at the centre of the world. The moats round the main building are the oceans, and the outer walls are the mountains supposed to surround the earth.

One of the great Moslem cities on the trade route to China was Samarkand, now in the USSR. This is one of three madrasahs or colleges of learning on the square called the Reghistan. It is covered with patterned tiles, some with pictures of living creatures, usually forbidden in the Moslem religion. Moslem architects delighted in geometrical patterns.

Ely Cathedral was begun in 1083 and finished in 1534. It is an example of Gothic architecture. The first tower collapsed in the 14th century and was replaced by one topped with an eight-sided lantern admitting light through its windows and roofed by a dome, the only Gothic dome in existence.

Height is achieved in Lincoln Cathedral by means of the pointed arch. The meeting of arches in the roof of the central nave supporting it is called fan vaulting.

This more modest church at Capel-y-ffin in Wales, is little more than an ordinary cottage with a belltower attached to one end.

The tower of the Horyu-ji Buddhist temple in Japan is of that peculiarly eastern design called a pagoda. Like the towers in the architecture of all great religions, it is meant to be seen from a distance by the faithful. This 7th century temple is the world's oldest monumental wooden building.

Among massive structures that have lasted through the centuries are fortified buildings. Castles were built where they could be easily defended. Eilean Donan castle stands on a small island in the Scottish Highlands, linked to the mainland by a narrow bridge which a handful of soldiers could defend.

People of wealth or position have often displayed their importance in the palaces designed for them. In 1815, John Nash redesigned the Royal Pavilion in Brighton for the Prince Regent who became George IV. Iron was then becoming popular as a building material. There are 61 tonnes (60 tons) of iron in the domes and the kitchen roof is supported on iron pillars. The style is based on Indian architecture. More palaces are shown on pages 94 and 95.

A palace was designed for Charles I in Whitehall by one of Britain's greatest architects, Inigo Jones. This banqueting hall was the only part which was actually built, between 1619 and 1622. This style of architecture began in Italy in the period called the Renaissance. It was a time when Europe awoke from the Dark Ages and the study of science and the arts was reborn. People were interested in ancient times, as the Greek pillars show.

The Royal Palace in Madrid has this room decorated with Italian porcelain in designs copied from the Chinese. The work was done about 1765 for the Spanish king, Charles III. He had a similar room in his summer palace. This highly decorative style, which began in France, is called rococo. It spread quickly through Europe, even into Russia. Pottery imported from China had created a taste for eastern art.

The Greeks of 3500 years ago built huge fortified palaces, as here at Tiryns. This passage, inside a 10-metre (32 feet 9·5 inches) thick outer wall, is roofed with overlapping stones in an old type of vaulting called corbelling.

Our knowledge of how people lived in the past comes mainly from their writings and pictures. Only rarely are there places where little has changed over the centuries. We are learning to preserve them, as in the Suffolk village of Lavenham. These houses are modernized inside, but only repaired on the outside to preserve their original appearance. A visit to Lavenham is like stepping back in history. The way in which private dwellings have changed over the years is illustrated here and on the next three pages.

▶ This is Jacques Coeur's house in Bourges, France. In the 15th century, he grew so rich that he controlled most of France's trade, even lending money to the king. His initials and coat-of-arms are used in a lot of the Gothic decoration.

▶ One of the great 16th century architects was the Italian, Andrea Palladio. Like many artists of his day, he was interested in ancient times, but he went too far in thinking that the design of ancient temples was suitable for private houses. This is his idea of a Roman villa. Palladian architecture spread through Europe and was popular for more than a century.

In 17th century France, classical architecture took on a new look from the designs of Francois Mansart. This house has no Greek pillars, but their lines are suggested in two-colour stone. He made roofs steeper and chimneys even higher. Gardens laid out in formal patterns also became popular about this time.

This is Longfellow House in Cambridge, Massachusetts, in the USA. Built in 1759, it was used by George Washington as his headquarters during the War of American Independence from British rule. It shows how the well-to-do American adapted the style of the English manor house. Greek-style pillars are there, but weatherproofed wooden boarding is used instead of stone. A similar house in the south would have the wooden pillars supporting a portico and balcony to shade the windows from the hot sunshine.

Frank Lloyd Wright became the leading American architect during the first half of the 20th century. His writing and teaching influenced other architects as much as the buildings he designed. Most of these were private houses. He believed that a house should become part of its surroundings. His most famous house is the Falling Water house at Bear Run, Pennsylvania. Here it is seen in winter with the waterfall frozen.

Now that people live in smaller spaces, grand designs have given way to all sorts of experiments. This building in Montreal is called Habitat housing. It is made of prefabricated living units that can be fitted together into almost any shape. Units can be added or removed, so that the shape of the building changes with the needs of the people living in it.

▶ As the Gothic architecture of medieval cathedrals gave way to the Renaissance style, the Roman arch appeared again. Its revival was due largely to Italian architect Filippo Brunelleschi who designed this Foundling Hospital in Florence in 1419. Here, in the courtyard, the Roman arch is used to support a main wall and not just the roof, as in Roman times. This picture shows how even an orphanage could be a beautiful building in those days.

▼ Public buildings, such as theatres, offices, even hospitals, are often designed to give a feeling of luxury rather than to suggest their purpose. The Paris Opéra looks more like a palace of an earlier age than a 19th century theatre. The main staircase is made of Algerian onyx, an ornamental stone, and everywhere elaborate decoration and costly materials add to the sense of luxury. The architect, Charles Garnier, also designed blocks of flats to make people feel they lived in a palace.

This Greek theatre at Epidauros was built in the 4th century BC and is still in use. The circular design solved the problem of seating a large audience just as a modern sports stadium does.

The geodesic dome, designed by Buckminster Fuller in 1967, is architecture brought back to the simplicity of a Greek theatre. It is just a protective shield for any internal arrangement.

Modern architects have made space for large numbers of people by inventing the skyscraper. Often, it is just an ugly filing cabinet, treating people as objects to be stowed neatly out of the way. Here, in the Lake Point Tower in Chicago, steel and glass have been used to give the building its shape and to reflect light like a jewel.

The Chrysler Building in New York was built in 1929 and was the first skyscraper to reach over 304·8 metres (1000 feet). The architect, William van Allen, was one of the first to use aluminium and stainless steel in a building. The picture shows only the top of the tower, which has the look, perhaps, of a space rocket, with its streamlined shape and sunburst pattern. This style was meant to suggest the machine age, when the idea of a world run smoothly by machinery was still new and exciting. Even now, it looks more modern than many more modern buildings do.

TRANSPORT

We can visit many of the world's wonders in a single lifetime because we have modern transport systems. It wasn't always so. Early man had to walk across the land and swim across the waters. Even when he had invented the wheel, the paddle and the sail, his travels were slow. He had only his own strength or the strength of beasts he could tame to pull his carts. No beast could be taught to ply a paddle or pull an oar. The sails of ships had to wait upon the wind.

Even so, great journeys were made. Ships sailed around the globe. New continents were discovered and explored. At last, a mere two hundred years ago, came the new sources of power. Steam drove mighty ships across the oceans. Railway tracks were laid across continents. Then oil and electricity took over from steam. The petrol engine speeds us along the motorways. It carries us soaring into the air.

The transport age has brought the whole world within easy reach and made neighbours of all mankind.

◄ As each new country was discovered and settlers moved in, the steam locomotive opened up the heartlands. Track was laid over every obstacle or tunnels driven through them. Here a freight train rattles across a river bridge in Arthur's Pass in New Zealand's South Island.

In the 16th century, seamen like Sir Francis Drake sailed seas where none had gone before them. Drake's Golden Hind, between 1577 and 1580, was the first English ship to sail round the world. This one is a modern reconstruction of the Golden Hind sailing today.

▼ The first known sailing ships were in ancient Egypt. Sails were particularly useful on the River Nile where the wind often blows from the north against the flow of the current. This modern Arab dhow has changed little since ancient times.

▲ The Chinese had their own kind of ship called a junk, with sails often made of split bamboo. This modern vessel has copied the shape of sail of the age-old junk.

Sailing ships reached their peak of speed in clippers, bringing tea from China and grain from Australia. They raced each other to be first home with their cargoes. This modern version of a clipper is a Polish training ship.

▲ The first steamships were paddleboats. The engines drove the great paddlewheels either at the stern or on either side amidships. This is a sternwheeler on the great Mississippi river in the USA. She was built in Scotland and shipped in pieces to California in 1926 where she ran a ferry service before moving to the Mississippi.

▼ The paddlewheel was soon replaced in most steamships. More speed and power could be got from propellers placed underwater beneath the stern. It took longer for the steam engine to give way to the oil-burning engine. Today, all great liners run on oil. This is the West German cruise ship Hamburg, built in 1969.

▲ The first steam railway locomotives were used for hauling coal. This is the famous Puffing Billy, built in 1813 and still in use at Wylam Colliery 50 years later.

Early public railways owed a lot to the father and son partnership of George and Robert Stephenson. Their Stockton to Darlington railway carried the first 600 passengers, in wagons towed by their engine, Locomotion, on the opening day in 1825. The locomotive Ixion was built by Daniel Gooch in 1841, based on earlier Stephenson designs. The picture shows a model of Ixion.

Steam railways quickly spread to the USA. They were a boon in such a big country where the cities were so far apart. This is a model of a locomotive built in 1843 by the Philadelphia engineer William Norris. The four front wheels swivel on a separate chassis so that the engine could manage steep inclines and sharp curves without coming off the rails.

▲ Hokkaido is the most northerly of Japan's islands, the least populated and the most thickly forested. Here in the mountains between the port of Hakodate and the capital, Sapporo, winter snow lies more than 1 metre (3 feet 3 inches) thick. Only continual work with snow ploughs keeps the line open. Two locomotives are needed to bring the express through.

▶ This is the view from the second tender of the Mossel Bay-to-Johannesburg express in South Africa. At Jagpoort, the leading engine is shunted round to the back to help push the coaches up the steep gradient of the Lootsberg Pass. At the top, the pusher locomotive is dropped off and the express continues its journey to the coast.

Increased traffic has made South African Railways switch to electrification or diesel on many lines. Here in the northern Transvaal, bigger steam engines and longer trains are used. 25 kilometres (15·54 miles) of winding track lead up to the Highveld, a rise of 1500 metres (5000 feet).

Goods for transport by road, sea and railway are nowadays usually packed into containers. These are like huge boxes that can be loaded and off-loaded easily from one kind of transport to another. The inset picture shows one of the big gantry cranes lifting a container from a road vehicle on to a 'freightliner' train of British Rail. This same container may already have been brought to Britain by ship with its contents undisturbed during the whole journey.

The Canadian Pacific Railway with its shipping and airways interests is the world's biggest transport system. The source of power for most of its locomotives is now diesel oil. The diesel engine, which is like a motor car engine, is usually used to make electricity for electric motors that actually turn the wheels. Here, a Canadian Pacific freight train emerges from the Red Sucker Tunnel in Ontario.

The extra turning power of an electric motor has often been useful on steep hills. Steam trains carrying freight across New Zealand's South Island (see pages 104 and 105), used to be switched to this three-unit electric locomotive to get them through the tunnel at the top of Arthur's Pass. Today, the battle is fought with diesel locomotives.

The Grand Canyon, a diesel locomotive of the Santa Fé Railroad, leaves Chicago's Dearborn Station on the long haul to Los Angeles. Privately owned passenger services like this have disappeared with the competition from cars and aircraft. Amtrack, the national company, operates all that still remain.

This is an experimental suburban line train of British Rail. It led to the development of a locomotive that could pick up an electric current either from a third rail or from overhead cables.

▲ Motor cars bring personal transport within reach of everyone. From the start, drivers challenged each other to races. This 1899 Canstatt-Daimler was one of the first cars specially built for racing.

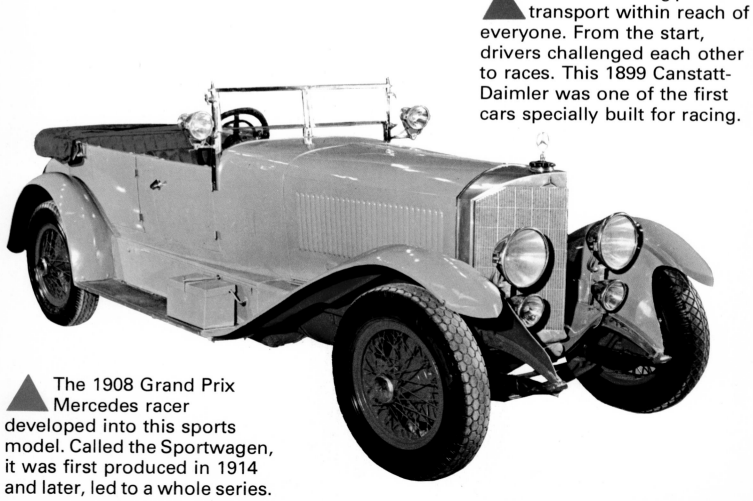

▲ The 1908 Grand Prix Mercedes racer developed into this sports model. Called the Sportwagen, it was first produced in 1914 and later, led to a whole series.

▲ This Ferrari Dino 246 GT is one in a long line of famous sports cars. Its elegant streamlining is typical of the best Italian design. The days when fast cars like this were kings of the road may be over now that speed limits have been fixed on most of the world's motorways.

▼ Excitement can be found by daredevil drivers in the motor rally. Rallying has recently become a popular sport. Some rugged country has been chosen for it. The East Africa Safari Rally is one of the toughest with poor roads, floods and wild animals. This Peugeot almost takes off as it hits a bump in the dirt road.

▲ The invention of the petrol engine provided a power unit light enough for a flying machine. Air transport could progress at last. This is a copy of an early pioneering aircraft designed by the American Glenn Curtiss, used as a World War I trainer.

▼ Many early flying machines were little more than kites on wheels. The petrol engine turned a propeller to give the aircraft enough speed to lift off from the ground. This is a copy of the 1910 Bristol Box-kite.

One problem with aircraft is to provide a runway long enough for take-off. Several ways have been tried to make an aircraft that can leap into the air from a standing start. This one has swivelling wings so that the propellers point upwards. These lift the aircraft like the rotorblades of a helicopter. Then the wings swivel back into the horizontal for level flight.

Some odd-looking aircraft have been built to carry big cargoes. This one has the lower fuselage, wings, tail and cockpit of a Boeing propeller airliner. Bits of other aircraft have been added on top to make a bigger cabin space. It is called the Guppy because it looks like the tropical fish popular in aquariums.

▶ Flying between the world's great cities has become commonplace. Journeys that, not so many years ago, took days are now made in a few hours. It often takes longer to get from the airport to the city centre or a neighbouring town than the actual flying time. Transport systems are trying to fill in the gaps where there is no handy airport for the bigger airliners. This de Havilland twin Otter is small enough to set down its passengers even in a meadow. It can carry people, freight and mail to remote areas where the population would otherwise be cut off from the rest of the world.

▼ Using a stretch of water as a runway for the take-off of an aircraft was tried from the very earliest pioneering days. Eventually, huge flying boats were built. The trouble was that they could not be used in rough weather. Nowadays, aircraft that land on water, like this Cessna floatplane, are usually small pleasure machines. They are useful, for instance, for the fisherman who wants to get away from it all to the distant mountain lakes, as here on Lake Mavora in New Zealand.

Small aircraft are being used more and more worldwide to help the farmer. They are designed to land and take off from small spaces. They can be fitted with sprays to spread weedkiller or fertilizer. They are even used for herding cattle or sheep. This handy little aircraft is the American Rockwell Quail Commander.

Nature invented the helicopter by putting a pair of wings on a seed. As the seed falls, its passage through the air makes the wings rotate so that the seed floats some distance before it settles. The first successful helicopter, built in Germany in 1936, had two sets of rotary blades. This overcame the problem of a single set making the whole aircraft spin in the air. In 1940, Igor Sikorsky fitted a propeller to the tail of a single-rotor helicopter, to counteract the spin. This twin-rotor Labrador is used for search and rescue work.

Aircraft that can travel faster than sound were the obvious next step after the invention of the jet engine. They are called supersonic, meaning above (or faster than) sound. At first, they were made for war, as fighters and bombers. The first supersonic passenger aircraft in the western world is the Concorde, designed and built by the British and French together. Its long pointed snout hides the pilot's view of the runway on the ground, so it is made to dip on take off and landing. It cruises at over 2330 kilometres (1500 miles) per hour.

SPORTS AND PASTIMES

Machines have been invented to work for us and to give us more leisure. But machines need looking after and take up a lot of our working time. For some, therefore, weekends and holidays are opportunities to leave machinery far behind for sports and pastimes such as sailing, horse riding and walking in the countryside. For others, machines are for pleasure, too, and for them the thrill of watching high-powered racing cars in action or flying light aircraft are ideal ways to spend free time.

◀ The wind skims across the bay. The sails fill and billow out. The race is on! These cruiser yachts in Australian waters provide exhilarating sport for the crews and a marvellous sight for onlookers.

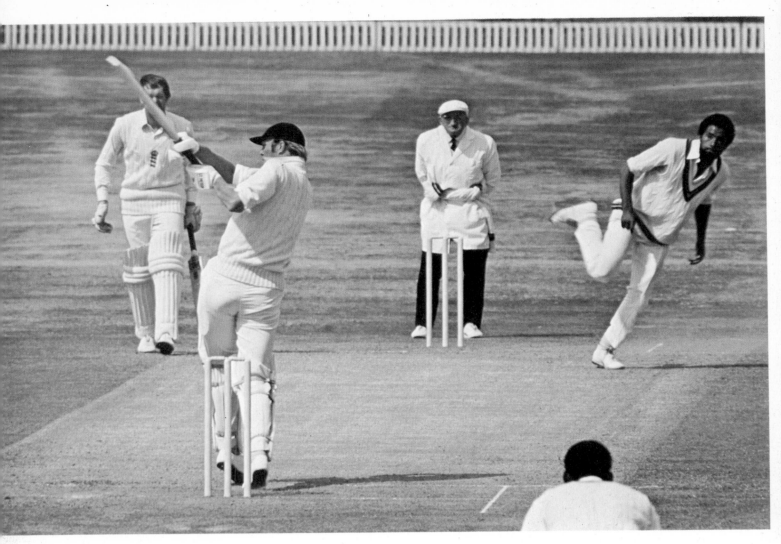

Games that involve striking a ball with some sort of stick or bat go back to ancient times. Cricket probably got its name from the Anglo-Saxon word for a shepherd's staff, *cricc*. A form of cricket was played by shepherds in England, using this staff as a bat and a wicket-gate from a sheep pen as the bowler's target. Until about 1770, cricket bats retained the curved shape of the shepherd's *cricc*. Then they began to straighten out into the shape of the modern cricket bat. It was also in the 1770s that the two stumps of early wickets were increased to three. The picture shows a test match at Headingley near Leeds, with Greig hooking a ball from Roberts.

Football is probably the oldest of all the games popular today. It was played by the ancient Greeks and Romans. Perhaps, the Romans brought it to Britain, though the first known account of it here dates back only to AD 1175. Shrove Tuesday was a popular day for a football match, when whole towns played against each other through the streets. There were no particular rules and the game became so rough it had to be banned in 1314. A code of rules was first written in 1846 at Cambridge University, and in 1863 the Football Association began to take control. The picture shows a match between Manchester City and Queen's Park Rangers.

At one time, the back of a horse was a more comfortable and safer place for the traveller than inside a coach. Since the motor car arrived, the skill of horsemanship has been kept alive. Here, Harvey Smith on Johnny Walker clears the poles at the All-England Course at Hickstead, Surrey.

Games played with a ball are the oldest and most varied ever invented. Even team games allow the skill of the individual to be all-important. Polo combines skill of hand and eye with a popular pastime, horseriding. There are accounts of it played in Persia and Assam at least 2500 years ago. It became a popular game in India and was taken up by British army officers stationed there. It was introduced into Britain in 1869. It is a fast game, exciting both to the players and to spectators. The ponies seem to enjoy it, too!

Show jumping on television has encouraged many children to take up riding. Schools teach grooming and care of a pony as well as how to ride. There are pony clubs to join and competitions to enter. A whole holiday can be spent pony-trekking through the countryside.

Riding bareback, this young girl takes her skewbald pony for a paddle. Horses are fun-loving animals and make the best of companions. Skewbald means a coat of brown and white patches.

Horses were brought to America by the Spaniards who conquered Mexico. Their use of a deep saddle and reins held in one hand spread north to the cowboys. This horse is an American breed, an Appaloosa.

The sun slants through the trees. The woodland path is far from the din of traffic. The boy and his pony are at peace with the world. This kind of gentle riding through the countryside is called hacking.

▲ Ever since dogs and horses have worked for mankind, we have enjoyed watching them race. The greyhound is specially bred for speed. In 1876, a course was laid out with a mechanical hare to urge the dogs onward. Since then, greyhound racing has become a popular sport. Here, three greyhounds race at full speed, towards the winning post.

▼ Racing horses on the flat and over fences has become a worldwide industry. These jockeys take their mounts over a brush fence that barely slows them in their stride.

A sport that uses modern machinery is motor racing. For some drivers, it is more than a pastime. It is their highly-paid work. Manufacturers use it to improve the performance and fame of their ordinary cars. This is the March 707 driven by Helmut Kelleners in the Canadian-American Cup.

Here is world motor-racing champion, James Hunt, driving to victory in a Marlboro Maclaren in the Race of Champions at Brands Hatch in May 1977. Men like Hunt risk their lives to reach championship standard. What is learned from racing helps to make ordinary motoring safer.

▶ The Bembridge Sailing Club have their own design of racing yacht, known as the Bembridge Redwing. Here, a pair of Redwings scud across choppy coastal waters with the wind abeam in a closely run contest.

▼ The crew of an ocean-racing yacht must work closely as a team. Everyone has his allotted job, but everyone must be ready for any emergency. The picture shows something of their hard concentration just after the start of a round-the-buoys, off-shore race.

The Mirror dinghy is a popular sailing craft for all the family. The hull is pram form, with bow cut square and lifted higher out of the water than the stern. The tall sail is fixed to a long gaff attached to a shorter mast. With the two foresails, enough wind can be caught to give it an exciting turn of speed.

Since the first conquest of the air, enthusiasts have built their own aircraft. In Britain, the Popular Flying Association has spread successful designs by its members. This Taylor Monoplane, designed by John Taylor, has been built from his plans by amateur fliers all over the world.

This single-seater sporting biplane was designed by the Experimental Aircraft Association in America. Aircraft like the ones on these pages can often be bought in kits to be made at home. There is great excitment in taking to the air in a home-made machine.

This American designed Airmark Cassutt was first built in Britain in 1969 to encourage air racing as a sport. It has a Rolls Royce engine giving a level speed of 315 kilometres (195 miles) per hour.

One of the simplest of all modern flying machines is this Aerosport Rail. It is safe and easy to fly, and has a top speed of 153 kilometres (95 miles) per hour.

Even rotary-wing aircraft can be bought in kits, like this Bensen Gyro-Copter. It has broken several speed and altitude records for its type.

THE WORLD OF BEAUTIFUL THINGS

We enjoy natural beauty: a vivid sunset, a carpet of flowers or the mist rising from a distant mountain. Some people, artists and craftsmen make beautiful things, often reflecting in their work the beauty of the natural world around them.

Creative men and women have been employed to design most of the things we buy. If we think of our homes we should probably find many, quite ordinary things that are pleasing to look at and use. An old chair, a pretty jug, a simple wooden cooking spoon. Printers, binders, editors and photographers have combined their skills to try to make this book beautiful.

In this part of the book you will find some of the beautiful things man has created, some of them dating back for centuries.

▶ Colour is one of nature's gifts to us. The way an artist uses colour can turn an ordinary object into something of dazzling beauty. A very skilled craftsman coloured the glass of this vase while it was being made in Austria in 1900.

▲ Pictures often tell a story. This painting of geese is from an ancient Egyptian tomb. The ancient Egyptians believed that a goose, the 'great cackler', laid an egg from which Ra, the sun god, was hatched. It was Ra who created the living world. Modern scientists also believe that the sun created life (see page 30).

◀ This is a portrait of Nefertari, wife of the Pharaoh Rameses II. He was one of ancient Egypt's great builders. Outside the rock temples of Abu Simbel are four statues of him, each almost 20 metres (65 feet) high. The name Nefertari means 'beautiful friend'. She had a tomb of her own, its walls covered in beautiful paintings like this one.

This is a bronze statue of the cat goddess Bast. The ancient Egyptians thought of the sun sailing in a ship across the heavens. Bast was supposed to go with it when it sailed out of sight at night. Each night, she fought off the serpent Apep, enemy of the sun god Ra, so that his ship could sail back over the world next morning. Cats were kept by the ancient Egyptians to protect them from snakes. This may have given them the idea for the story.

The ancient Greek hero, Heracles, was given twelve Labours by Eurystheus, king of Tiryns (see page 94). One was to capture a stag with brass hoofs and gold horns. He hunted it for a year before he succeeded. This vase painting shows him breaking off a gold horn, watched by goddesses, Athene and Artemis.

This sculpture by Bernini (1598–1680) shows the ancient Roman god Jupiter as a baby looked after by a mountain nymph and a goat. When one of the goat's horns fell off, it was full of fruit, a cornucopia or horn of plenty. The goat Capra and the horn (corn) became the stars of the constellation Capricorn.

▼ Ancient Roman artists liked to show rivers, cities and even whole continents as people in their pictures. This picture, from a villa in Sicily, shows Africa as a woman. She holds an elephant tusk in one hand and palm tree in the other, and is surrounded by her animals. The bird rising from the flames on the left is the legendary bird, the phoenix. This sort of picture is a mosaic, made from tiny pieces of coloured stone cemented to a floor or wall.

▲ Pictures can tell stories from the Bible, like this one of Jonah from a monastery in Turkey. Jonah was caught in a storm at sea. The sailors blamed him for the storm and threw him overboard. A great fish swallowed him, carried him to the shore and left him safe on dry land.

◀ This 12th century painting from a church in Switzerland illustrates a miracle story from the New Testament. When some of Christ's disciples went fishing, they caught nothing. Jesus called to them from the shore to cast their nets on the other side of the boat. The net was filled at once.

One of the great glories of medieval churches and cathedrals is their stained glass windows. From inside the building, the glass pictures are lit up by the sunshine outside. No modern artists have been able quite to match the brilliant colours of the early glassmakers. This old window shows Noah in his Ark. The dove has just returned with an olive branch in its beak, proving that dry land is near.

The success of Meissen porcelain, made by a new process invented by J. F. Böttger about 1710, started great rivalry between the princes of Europe. Louis XV of France opened a factory at Sèvres where this wine cooler was made in 1784.

These tobacco jars are stoneware, a common clay fired at high temperatures. Beside the jars are pressers to keep the tobacco firm and moist. The figure is French biscuit, unglazed porcelain with no shine on it.

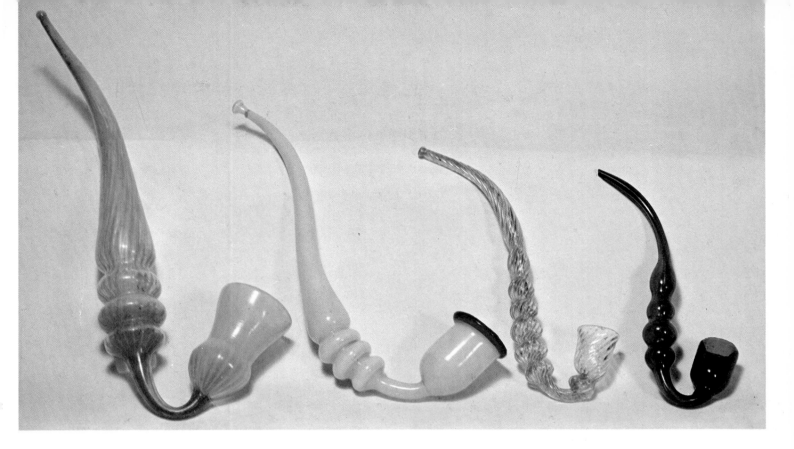

Pipes for smoking tobacco have been made from wood, clay, metal and stone. These delicate and beautifully made glass pipes were not very practical. They were made during the first half of the 19th century for tobacconists to display in their shop windows. Glass has long been used for display and ornamental purposes because of the way it reflects light.

In the arts and crafts, China has always been at least the equal of other civilizations. In pottery, it has hardly been bettered. When Chinese pottery appeared all over Europe in the 16th century, the fine white porcelain, so fine that the light shone through it, was most admired. European factories tried hard to match it. Even the name 'china' was adopted for fine porcelain. This 'Dog of Fo' was a favourite subject for Chinese artists of the time. This one was made in porcelain about 1700. It looks like the Chinese breed of lion dog or Pekinese.

▼ Artists and craftsmen of the 16th century invented a heavy and elaborate style of decoration called baroque. Chairs in this style were more like royal thrones. Everyday furniture was simpler, like these chairs with straight arms and square legs but even these were enriched with upholstery of fine tapestry woven into pictures and patterns. It shows the high quality of this upholstery that it has lasted so long. When an object is beautiful then, of course, people will take more care of it.

▶ It is thought that the art of making knotted carpets began in Turkey and Persia. From there, it spread north into Russia, south to Egypt and east to India. Perhaps it reached China, or it may have been invented there quite independently. Only the canvas backing is woven. The coloured wools or silks are knotted on to it one tuft at a time. The design is drawn on squared paper. Once it was drawn in sand or made into a song for the weaver to memorise it. This 19th century silk rug comes from Turkey.

This 19th century bed, designed by the architect William Burges, is based on medieval designs. Not only has the craft of the woodworker been used to the full, the bed has also been richly decorated by a painter. Furniture like this and the painted cupboards can be admired as beautiful objects quite apart from the use made of them.

This desk was made by J. H. Riesener in France during the reign of Louix XVI. The metalwork fixed to the wood is a feature of this period. It was usually a mixture of brass, copper and zinc giving a golden-yellow colour. It was shaped in delicate patterns, often to look like leaves or ribbons. It was called ormolu.

Here is an example of one art giving inspiration to another. The ancient Greeks painted pictures on their vases (see page 144) which often included furniture. This couch, with its scroll ends and back, was made in the early 19th century. Its design is based on couches seen on the Greek pottery. It exactly suited the romantic ideas of elegant ladies who saw themselves as the new Greeks with their love of luxury and the arts.

The Casimir Bru factory in France was famous for its dolls. Some made crying noises, some took milk from a bottle and some could be seen to breathe. Some had two faces that could be swivelled to show the doll laughing or asleep. The biggest of these has a china face and arms with a leather body. The others have jointed wooden limbs and bodies. Dolls like these are works of art. The French used dolls to advertise the latest fashions. There was a long tradition of doll dressmakers skilled at including every detail of lacework and fine stitching in miniature.

Toys don't often last long but this doll is over 100 years old! She seems, perhaps, too delicate to play with. She has beautifully kept hair with the original ribbon. The lace on her muslin dress is handmade.

Here is a very grown up doll dressed in the fashion of a century ago when she was made. The fur muff she holds is both a handwarmer and a pocket. Fashion dolls have become popular again nowadays.

Acknowledgements

The Publishers would like to thank the following individuals and organisations for their kind permission to reproduce the photographs in this book.

A–Z Botanical Collection Ltd 38 above, 44 below; AFSEN 25; Air Portraits 138 below; Malcolm Aird 90 below left; Bernard Alfieri 51; Heather Angel 24 above; Ardea (D. Avon & T. Tilford) 72 above, 74 below (I. R. Beames) 81 (H. & J. Beste) 83 right (R. Bunge) 75 above (K. Fink) 72 below (A. Weaving) 74 above; Anthony Bannister 64, 68, 71, above; Barnaby's Picture Library 12 above, 14 right; Bavaria Verlag 15 above; Beken of Cowes 106, 107 above and 7 below, 108; John Bethell 90 above left; Bille 69 below; Biofotos 36; Alistair Black 137; Almenna Bokafelagid 13; Pat Brindley 48–49, 55 left; British Aircraft Corporation 121 above; British Museum (Natural History) (photo: Imitor) 20, 21 left and below right, 56, 57 above and 6; British Tourist Authority 90 right; British Transport Films 115 inset, 117 below; D. Calkin 2–3; Camera Press Ltd 82; Canadian Pacific 114–115; J. Allan Cash Ltd 14–15; John Cleare 4–5; Roger Fresco Corbu 148 below, 149 above and below; Ben Cropp 61 below, 63 above; Anne Cumbers 30–31; Daily Telegraph Colour Library 136 below left; P. M. David 23, 62 below; W. F. Davidson 33 below; De Beers 16 below; K. Desmonde (photo: Angelo Hornak) 154 above and below, 155; Deutsche Atlantic Line 109 below; Ron Dorman 126–127; Patrick Eager 128; Werner Forman Archive 89; J. Good 79 above; A. G. C. Grandison 69 above, 70 below; Greyhound Racing Association 134 above; Noel Habgood 92–93; Sonia Halliday 94 above, 102 above, 145, 146 above and below, 147; Victor Hand 104–105, 112 above and below, 113, 116, 117 above; Peter Hill 24 below; Michael Holford Library 16 above left and above right, 86 above, 93, 143, 144 above; Angelo Hornak 98 right, 100–101, 103 left and right, 152–153; G. E. Hyde 50; Institute of Geological Sciences, London 14 left, 17, 19 below; Instituto Vendite Guidiziarie, Florence 150; Jacana Agence de Presse (W. Schraml) 79 below; A. F. Kersting 95, 100; Albert Klein 148 above; Gerold Kalt 135 above; E. D. Lacey 130 above, 134 below; Howard Levy 138 above left and above right, 139; W. MacQuitty 142 below; Leo Mason 129, 135 below; G. Mazza 32; J. Meads 131; John Moss 130 below; N.H.P.A. (H. R. Allen) 40 above, 42, 43 (D. Baglin) 73 (Anthony Bannister) 66 above and below (Bruce Barnetson) 61 above (N. A. Callow) 67 above and 7 above (J. M. Clayton) 26, 27 above and below, 28 above and below, 29 (Stephen Dalton) 67 below, 75 below, 78 above (Valerie Finnis) 44 above (Anthony Huxley) 38 below (G. E. Hyde) 34 above, 35 above (L. H. Newman) 35 below (Ivan Polunin) 46 (M. Savonius) 40 below (Roy Shaw) 39 (M. W. F. Tweedie) 65 above and below (G. Wall) 34 below; Natural Science Photos 57 below, 58, 59; Perez (London) Ltd 151; Photoaquatics 21 above right; Photo Resources 37; Pictorial Press Ltd 80; Picturepoint Ltd 76–77, 83 left, 99 above, 102 below, 107 below; E. H. Rao 70 above; Peter Roberts 118 above and below, 119 above and below; Iantha Ruthven 133; Keith Sagar 60, 62 above, 63 below; Scala 84–85, 87 above, 144 below; Kenneth Scowan 49; The Director, The Science Museum, London 110, 111 above and below; Bruce Scott 77 above; G. T. Seurin 109 above; Roger Smith 136 above; Harry Smith Horticultural Photographic Collection 41, 45, 47, 52 above and below, 54 above and below; Spectrum Colour Library 33 above, 53, 87 below; Margie Spence 132 above; T. Stack 71 below; Sutton's Seeds 55 right; J. W. R. Taylor 121 below, 122, 124 above and below, 139 above; J. W. R. Taylor and M. J. H. Taylor 120 above and below, 123, 125; S. A. Thompson 132 below; Victoria & Albert Museum (A. C. Cooper) 152 above; Waddesdon Manor (Photo: Angelo Hornak) 153 above; Weidenfeld & Nicholson 88 above and below, 91 (Kenny Durdas) 94 below (Ian Graham) 86 below, 97 above and below, 98 left; Western Pennsylvania Conservancy, Pittsburgh 99 below; D. P. Wilson 22 below; Roger Wood Studio 142 above; Trevor Wood 96–97; ZEFA Picture Library 10–11, 12 below (Hemlinger) 18 (W. H. Muller) 78 below (E. Sylvester) 22 above.